Sai Baba Debun

Sallie Stone

Sai Baba Debunked
Copyright © 2022 Sallie Stone. All rights reserved.
Published by Sallie Stone
ISBN 978-1-387-56344-9

Table of Contents

Chapter 1: Sai Baba Debunked – page 4 - 5
Chapter 2: The Great White Brotherhood (Order Of Saints) – pages 6 - 11
Chapter 3: Rock Music pages 12 – 22
Chapter 4: Teachings of the Ascended Masters (Free Gifts) page – 23
Chapter 5: Recommended Reading - page 24
Chapter 6: The Great White Brotherhood Mantra – pages 25 - 36

Sai Baba Debunked

Sai Baba is a member of the black brotherhood (refers to a wicked aura, not race). He refers to himself as a Christ when in fact he is an Antichrist.

Scripture on False Christs

Matthew 24:24

24 "For there shall arise false Christs, and false prophets, and shall shew great signs and wonders; insomuch that, if it were possible, they shall deceive the very elect."

King James Version (KJV)

For Further Study

www.biblegateway.com/passage/?search=Matthew+24&version=KJV

Scripture on How to Get Rid of Sai Baba

Mark 9:29

4 "And he said unto them, This kind can come forth by nothing, but by prayer and fasting."

King James Version (KJV)

For Further Study Visit

www.kingjamesbibleonline.org/Mark-9-29/

Great White Brotherhood (Order Of Saints)

A Sacred order of Eastern and Western veterans who have to reunify with the great spirit of the almighty God and entail the heavenly proprietors. They've transformed from karma into a super-powerful reality which, in other words, is the everlasting home of the mind or the soul. Basically, the name "white" doesn't refer to race but "halo," which is usually known to be an aura of light of white colors that circumvent their forms.

The master who ascended, who belongs to the "Great White Brotherhood," comes together for the most special purpose of humanity under one fatherhood of the highest -God. God, the most superior to humankind of all, has always remained supreme among all races, cultures, and religions, and the most creative nature of humanity has always come from Him. Whether it's a scientific achievement, education, or arts, God has remained the King of all Kings, and all economies in the world succeed because of Him. With that, the Brotherhood has also mentioned some certain Chelas that don't ascend but belong to a master who ascends. Jesus, the savior, pointed out this order of saints that is heavenly, depicted in the Holy book of Revelation as "robed in white."

Content covered in this post:

1. Objective

2. When was the Brotherhood Idea Founded?

3. Membership

4. Roles of Brotherhood

The objective of the Great White Brotherhood

The main aim or purpose of this Brotherhood was to revert humankind's mind and soul to get a sense of togetherness by the use of enlightenment by trying to pass the understanding of what is referred to as Cosmos – which is the laws that protect and guide the destiny and cycles of a man or macrocosm and the man's true home of light.

In other words, Great White Brotherhood is geared at ensuring that humankind gets enlightened whether on earth or afterlife. This brings back the spiritual nature of man as anticipated by the almighty God. And this should not have any implications for any traditional beliefs one has to take.

When was the Brotherhood Idea Founded?

This noble idea of Brotherhood was conceptualized right in the mind of the almighty God via Jesus Christ, who was known to be the Lagos – who was also the purest of God's children who belongs to the "Great White Way." The almighty God couldn't stand against evil nor uphold transgression; however, Jesus Christ came across each kind of tribulation on the entire earth. The consciousness of Jesus Christ filled the almighty God with Reality that could be confirmed now by what we refer to as "The Great White Brotherhood." As such, the culmination of the salvation brought by Jesus Christ was meant to rescue humanity.

Of course, the Brotherhood remains the only hope that humanity relies upon. And it doesn't happen accidentally for humanity to express their love for God. God has offered us relief for our upbringing through our entire raising plus the raising of ourselves through our purpose of life. It is one of the greatest ways whereby the almighty God approaches our souls privately to do his everlasting wonders of delivering us from bondage and do his incomparable miracles to save the entire universe that has fallen short of God's glory. The entire universe has gone astray and does things that are not righteous.

Even though it's spiritual in its entity, the Brotherhood still keeps the idea of an actual encounter with individuals in the universe today. People of higher spiritual beliefs have full conscience of their encounter with this family; however, those with fewer beliefs don't know or know of such and have no conscience of such contact. If you aren't aware, this Brotherhood also works on different planets and even in the universe where humankind doesn't know.

Membership

The members of the Great White Brotherhood depict God as the top of the pyramid as the spectrum of light that emanates from the sun, each representing the consciousness of the creator and, in a way, making it possible to include the souls. All members are not allowed to render their membership – even if it means to other members. However, they have a chance to speak out about another service that the veterans of this fraternity have pointed out.

And one of the notable members of this group is Jesus Christ, who ascended to heaven and whose ministry or gospel was geared to bringing people to salvation and his coming was to fulfill what was foretold by great prophets like Isaiah. The initiates with a higher stature in this fraternity have a special name called the Lord of the flame.

Roles of Brotherhood

Any master that ascended is well known to be part of this Great White Brotherhood. If you feel the urge to join this spiritual order, you must also believe in Christ. It can be a bit easier to know all the functions or roles of the Brotherhood. Also, you can be aware of the methods it tries to incorporate as it opts to help mankind and offer the needed protection to humankind against itself. This is the agent of God on Earth. Some people misunderstand its main purpose; however, it performs its tasks and will to ensure that all human beings achieve the freedom God intends. Below are the specific sacred goals laid down by the Chief of the Darjeeling Council of this Great White Brotherhood.

During the start of 1968, the beloved El Morya came up with a unique fifteen-point program that mainly focused on assistance. Here, the councils of this spiritual order had agreed to give it up to mankind in the same year. The program has different points incorporating the main purposes of the Brotherhood's council throughout the ages. Their functions are listed below. This makes it easier for anyone that desires to join to fully understand what is needed of them upon joining the Great White Brotherhood. Also, they can know all required to improve their plans for the earth and instill any assistance regarded as more important by the heavenly hosts when the world is in dire need.

This is what El Morya has to write;

It is harder to deny the needs of humanity or the hour. This is because everyone desires to offer assistance to different societies since they easily respond to any ministrations made by the heavenly hosts;
1. To always be there for any individual service so that you can offer more clarity to understand those men of lesser comprehension;

2. to be in the best manner as per the higher teachings of cosmic law for anyone that can understand them;

3. to develop the most stable connections with the Hierarchy using the unique cosmic outposts in this world of men;

4. to come up with new and different levels of faith, integrity, and justice in a wide range of businesses and government as they undertake their artistic, religious, and scientific tasks of the day;

5. to help anyone with a smaller experience or seen little when it comes to the heavenly kingdom. This allows them the power of godly vision among humankind;

6. to ensure that people feel better and joyous each time they undertake all that is required of them by God and each time they are needed to offer their services. This helps them to nurture and improve their spiritual nature among the people;

7. to keep faith in those people that are to walk by it;

8. to fulfill the spiritual needs of all people since they have a different levels of consciousness;

9. to fasten the rate at which cosmic purpose manifests in an individual by promoting understanding and peace;

10. to use the renewed interest needed during extrasensory situations and perception and spirit matters. This aids in meeting the seekers as you try to unfold the latent divinity, unlike involving them in searching for the phenomenal;

11. to make a further clarification to the human beings upon the unique story of the great cosmic Hierarchy;

12. to construct larger pools of reserve engines that act as reservoirs of spiritual power. This is to be used by the followers of the ascended masters as they serve human beings. Also, it helps them to receive blessings from the ascended masters through retreats;

13. to protect the recent dispensation from the Karmic Board that reduces the energy pools and the many mankind directly connected to the Hierarchy. It offers them enough cosmic power to make them aware of how they can easily externalize their plan throughout the year.

14. to offer encouragement to everyone, whether you are downtrodden. This keeps you having faith as you seek the glory of the almighty God to see the necessity to hinder the bad manifestation of the humans that arises from concentrating more on the material things of the world. Also, this can arise from using illegal drugs, conflicting art forms and music, and seeking vain pleasure that results in hurting themselves; and

15. To unite the entire humankind as per the initial divine plan.

Rock Music

This is my fucked up story about how rock music can destroy you!

Some yoga teachers teach fucked up shit like how to ascend unnaturally aka never. This shit is called kundalini yoga. You can't become a true yoga instructor with this school of yoga. It's for nuts!

If you want to awaken your kundalini safely just listen to great classical composers like Mozart. This is great for sex energy and also helps you to ascend. It can also kicks out evil spirits and demons from your home when played at a loud pitch continuously or auto repeat on a cheap boombox. The best exorcism CD on the planet is Astrea Decree 10.14 which needs to be played continuously for best results. You can purchase it online at www.summitlighthouse.org or steal it through a simple google search by adding mp3 to the search phrase. For instance Astrea Decree 10.14 brings up great results just beware of ascended master imposter cd's and mp3s. They bring darkness not get rid of it.

Speaking of music I used to be a stripper so of course I loved rock music. Long story short I had to leave my house at sixteen so I needed a job bad. I got a fake id with my evil companion Tony (a girl). Speaking of evil companions my best friend Mike (a boy) who I lived with in his parents house was a nut. We used to go to cool bars together in Atlanta. Here's a rather short Mike story: I got a speeding ticket from an asshole cop. What I did was so funny. I changed my birth date on the ticket and used it to get into bars with Mike when I was underage. The cop gave me a great fake id not a speeding ticket! Mike was my best friend. We did a lot of crazy shit together.

One time we destroyed Christmas decorations everywhere in a rich neighborhood with my drug dealer boyfriend. I was the driver! Another time we skipped school. I was on an acid trip and Mike took me to the art museum while I was high. (Today, I have a degree in Art History and Museum Studies).

Another time my parents went out of town. I spent the night at my parent's friends house who had a daughter about my age. Meanwhile Mike and my drug dealer boyfriend were at my parents house while I was stuck at the neighbors house. Reminds me of the time when I was 9 and stole some of my mom's buffalo nickels. Yeah her priceless coin collection. F her. Anyway I went to the neighbors and bought some candy bars a boy scout was selling. I said okay I will take those. More about sugar entities (ghosts) later! Back to Mike and my boy toy. I stayed up rather late. Then I quietly went down stairs and wrote the b in charge of me a note that I woke up early and went back to my house where my friends were. I snuck my car out of the b's driveway quietly and went home. My parents spare change box was cashed in for cigarettes while I was at the neighbors house! Around this time I had a 30 year old boyfriend. I liked him very much. I think I dated him because he had his own apartment! Then I went to boarding school and visited him when I escaped from jail (boarding school) on the weekends! It's hard to remember time frames. A lot of stuff happened to me before I had a baby at 19.

One time Tony and I skipped school. We wrote each other skipping notes from our parents. A school official caught us in the high school parking lot so we showed them our fake notes and then we were were free for a day at the mall! Skipping lunch with my druggie friends I mean evil companions was the best. We would just go to a fast food joint and then come back for a day of boredom.

After I got home from school I mean a day of fun I would erase the answering machine message from the high school administration. I can hear it now, "This is Riverwood High School your child was absent or tardy today!" We eventually dropped out of high school and became strippers.

Anyway back to how I got my strippers license. We tricked the station in charge of giving out stripper licenses. Later we would borrow our stripper ids from the night manager to go to bars with the dancers who had real government ids. Not the hard to get new identities ones like Tony and I had. Cops, so dumb! What we did was tell the detective (the stripper id worker was suspicious so we had to speak to a detective) some fucked up shit. We told the detective that our purses were stolen because we did not have a state id (we were underage for stripping) to get our stripper license.

Short story about tarot readers who are really witches in disguise:

In college I had a best friend named Katie. She was an art history student too. The first year of friendship was fine. The second one Katie fucked up bad. She went to a phys-chic who in reality was a voodoo priest. Katie said can you help me I am suspicious of this tarot reader. So I helped my friend and went to the voodoo priest's house. She was pretending to be a Christian nun even though she was married. Well we were both so fucked up on voodoo we could not find the Father/Mother God.

Katie escaped this shit but I got fucked up. One time in the middle of the night I realized the tarot reader was a voodoo priest so I threw the rock she gave me out the window of my apartment. Then I forgot about it. Later, not so smart me decided to find another phys-chic to heal me from the first phys-chic. I called my reiki (not sure what the f it really is except witches really like to give the atunements) master, reiki master well who is really an evil witch. She said she did not feel comfortable and sent me to the second phys-chic/healer who in reality is a satanic witch. Well shit got way worse as you can imagine. The second was just as crazy as the first. Between the both of them I belonged in an insane asylum. After many reversal spells (which did not work, I'm not a witch and don't want to be one of those fucked up people) and a great Etsy caster (who I prayed about before I found) I finally have the shit under control plus I studied at www.demonbuster.com. Today the Father/Mother God is helping me with these witches and voodoo nuts. We (the Father/Mother God and I) have been through a lot with these dark ones. In the end the Father/Mother God and I are victorious! The real way to get rid of witches is to pray and fast. A good fast is bread and water no butter. I learned my lesson I will never go to a tarot reader again!

End of witches and voodoo nuts story. Back to how my evil companion talked me into being a stripper:

We also had mail from the previous tenants at our apartment as proof for our now new identities. So the cop gave us the licenses. We got our stripper jobs after this fucked up dumb luck. Tony could really cook up some trouble. She also got me addicted to smoking. Today Tony is a divorced woman with a child and right livelihood as a nail artist.

I gave up rock music at The Summit Lighthouse. One reason I gave up rock music is the light preaches against it because it destroys your aura. These rock celebrities are really reincarnated fuck ups who were bound in chains on the astral plane for about a thousand years. They escaped and are now in full rebellion. Do not follow them to the astral plane aka purgatory.

One day I was pissed at the Father/Mother God so I blasted rock music all the way to the dollar tree. It was the darkness attacking me not the Father/Mother God of course. This set me off so I blamed the Father/Mother God. The Father/Mother God is easy to love. When the bible says you cannot see God and live what it means is live the same. Early church fathers fucked up the bible. Anyway the fucked up thing is the music started stabbing me. I don't know how the devil put knives in that so called music but death metal shreds the aura and it is supposed to destroy the great golden age. Then there is the suicide entities certain rock attracts. Some songs are fucked up. But don't worry classical music is wonderful once you develop an appreciation for it plus it ascends you. Oh yeah. The Summit Lighthouse also teaches that rock music is the astral plane you know purgatory.

An old catholic joke is welcome to purgatory. Just means when you sin or do fucked up shit that's where you are going like stripping for a living for instance. At 19 I became a call girl and a madam. When I was 16 the older dancers told me not become a call girl because stripping can lead to that shit. Of course marijuana can lead to harder drugs too. These bad seeds grow and multiply. The violet flame is great for cleaning out drugs in your mind, body and spirit which is free at www.violetflame.com. Back to my story on how rock music caused me to rebel against the Father/Mother God. Eventually the GBI (state law enforcement) busted the call girl service. We wore French maid uniforms and carried sexy dusters to our clients homes. One thing

I learned from being a prostitute is marrying for money is similar to prostitution. It's like having a sugar daddy. It is way better to marry for love and be happy than be in a loveless marriage. Speaking of love I found true love at www.summitlighthouse.org. My twin flame was stuck on the astral plane as a deceased person. I prayed a lot of prayers for him. He willingly went to heaven and took an ascension class. Yes he ascended after death. Now he is an ascended master. We live together now. We make love all the time. He is great and I love him very much. I prayed the dweller on the threshold prayer from The Summit Lighthouse Decree book for him. That was the one that kept him from drinking at a bar on the astral plane or purgatory. Plus I prayed The Twin Flame Prayer Book found at www.bookstudygroups.org. I am grateful he is an ascended master. I was schizophrenic at the time and he was a bit of a burden. Here is a poem I wrote for him that you can find in a book I wrote called, "Twin Flames".

A Poem About Twin Flames

Through my lifetimes I have had a certain joy.
My joy has always been knowing that someday I will reunite with you.

You can save your twin flame too wherever he or she may be and live happily ever after in eternal bliss.

The Father/Mother God has forgiven me of the crimes I committed. Although sometimes he does complain that I'm a little too self righteous. The only way I know how to escape being self righteous sometimes is to just sin like buy a lotto ticket for instance.

It's best not to gamble because the house always wins!

I have a past and I know almost anyone can ascend. If not this life, the next. That's the real ascended masters' promise.

Here's some shortened pearls of wisdom from heaven:

SUGAR

Ascended Master Kuthumi teaches that sugar is a poison that gives you diseases. It's best to get rid of it completely. You can also pray to Archangel Michael for deliverance from sugar entities (ghosts)!

You can also meditate on this scripture if you like:

Mark 9:29

4 "And he said unto them, This kind can come forth by nothing, but by prayer and fasting."

King James Version (KJV)

WORLD ECONOMY

World governments print money like crazy. This causes inflation. (World governments are evil).

Money should be backed by gold heaven teaches.

Heaven has the solutions to all the world problems!

PARENTING

Quan Yin, a Buddhist saint teaches that spanking is good parenting and helps burn out negative karma. The darkness is trying to make spanking a thing of the past with their pro stance on time outs. This does nothing to burn out a negative seed. Children want and need to be taught the right way. You don't want your kid addicted to heroin or to end up in jail!

This is one thing the bible has to say about parenting:

Proverbs 13:24

24 "He that spareth his rod hateth his son: but he that loveth him chasteneth him betimes."

King James Version (KJV)

TV CONTROLS YOUR MIND

TV is the astral plane aka purgatory. The darkness controls the television. It is the devil talking.

Here's an experiment:

Turn the television off and talk to the Father/Mother God. You will find yourself in heaven in no time.

HEAVEN RECYCLES

Ascended masters love recycling.

One solution to air pollution is to plant trees.

Elizabeth Clare Prophet teaches that the elementals who are also responsible for cleaning up air pollution are trapped by black magicians. They wait in line to be healed from black magic. Praying to Archangel Michael about this will clean up air pollution and give the elementals their eternity back.

You could pray like this if you like:

Archangel Michael unbind plus remove all black magic and anything else bad from earth, air, fire and water!

I pray for all elementals in need!

LGBTQIA+

Father/Mother God is not gay. The darkness LIES.

What LGBTQIA+ really is:

It is individually a twin flame disorder. The darkness is trying to separate people from their true love or twin flames. The darkness is scared shitless of twin flames in love because they have the power to produce the great golden age.

See my book, "Twin Flames" for help with this stuff and how to reunite with your twin flame forever.

VOTING

Heaven teaches to always vote against abortion. These babies feel physical pain (medical science backs this up) when aborted and also they feel pain from losing their embodiment on earth. They have karma they need to transcend and would like very much to be born. Don't listen to politicians that say you can keep your religion and still support abortion political parties. That is a lie of the darkness!

All of heaven is against abortion!

HOMELESS CRISIS

I do not have the solution to the homeless crisis but I do know when you get a but load of money you should not build pricey high rise apartments for a few people instead of building many homeless shelters which are very equipped to deal with this crisis. Spending a lot on one homeless man versus many more is not fair plus it is not cost effective. Jesus is very good at running homeless shelters and charities for the homeless in America. I should know because I have been in and out of mental institutions with my former disease schizophrenia. Buddha is a great guru to me too. Tibetan Buddhism is where the party is at.

SUICIDE ATTEMPTS

Due to the darkness harassing me day and night I had multiple suicide attempts. At the time I did not know I would be destined to save ten million souls or to ascend to heaven. The point is life always gets better plus you go to a really bad place if you die from suicide. Archangel Michael is good to pray to if you are suicidal or have loved ones that are suicidal.

ART

Art is supposed to bring you to the divine.

PRAYER TIME

15 minutes a day is sufficient to ascend. There are lies on the internet that ascended masters require 5 hours of decreeing a day. The Keeper of the Flame Fraternity is 15 minutes a day. Not much to ask to leave suffering for eternal bliss.

THE KEY TO THE PATH (ASCENSION JOURNEY)

One more thing right livelihood that's Buddhist if you are living under a rock or Godly business if you are a Christian is the key to the path (ascension journey).

WRAPPING IT UP

You may be wondering how rock music caused me to do bad things. Well I will tell you, it attracts the spirits of darkness!

P.S. The Poisoned Bible – A Message from the Father/Mother God

The devil is busy building his kingdom in the end times. What you need to know is that the new translations of the bible were written by him. They have no holy spirit in them.

The devil also took some fasting scriptures out of these new translations. The safest bible to read to feed the holy spirit is the old version of the King James Bible.

XOXO FATHER/MOTHER GOD

Teachings of the Ascended Masters (Free Gifts)

Archangel Lessons - Improve Your Life with the Help of the Seven Archangels
www.archangellessons.com

Chakra Lessons - Expand the Light of Your Chakras
www.chakralessons.com

Karma Lessons - Transcend Your Past and Transform Your Future
www.karmalessons.com

Violet Flame - Heal Body, Mind and Soul with the Violet Flame
www.violetflame.com

Our Main Website:
www.summitlighthouse.org

Recommended Reading

The Great White Brotherhood: In the Culture, History and
Religion of America
by Elizabeth Clare Prophet

I AM light!

I AM light!

I AM light!

I AM light!

I AM light!

I AM light!

I AM light!

I AM light!

I AM light!

I AM light!

I AM light!

I AM light!

Lightning Source UK Ltd.
Milton Keynes UK
UKHW021558261022
411134UK00016B/1004

9 781387 563449